ROSAMUNDE PILCHER'S
Cornwall

Gill Knappett

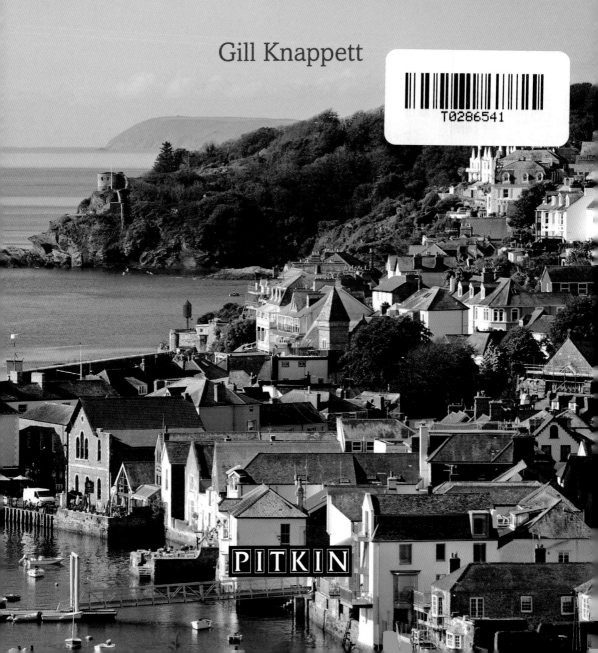

PITKIN

—ʼ— ROSAMUNDE PILCHER —ʼ—

The name Rosamunde Pilcher is intrinsically linked with one of England's most beautiful counties: Cornwall. Not only was this the county of her birth, but it became a focus for many of her novels, including the one that brought her international fame when it was published in 1987: it was, of course, *The Shell Seekers*.

Rosamunde Scott was born in Lelant, close to St Ives, in 1924, where the gardens of her childhood home ran down to Lelant railway station. Schoolgirl Rosamunde found it hard to leave Cornwall – 'paradise for us children' as she later remarked – and relocate to Wales with her family when her father, an officer in the Royal Navy, was posted there during the Second World War. On leaving school she attended secretarial college in Gloucestershire; like her beloved Cornwall, the Cotswolds, which she enjoyed exploring on long bicycle rides, were to feature in *The Shell Seekers*.

Rosamunde Pilcher at a book-signing in 2012

She later joined the Navy and in 1945, whilst serving as a Wren, *Woman & Home* magazine published one of her short stories, for which she received 15 guineas. The following year she married Graham Pilcher, a Scottish army officer whom she met at a party in St Ives. The young couple moved to Scotland and had four children.

Rosamunde continued writing and her first book – a Mills and Boon romance – was published in 1949 under the pseudonym Jane Fraser. She already had several novels and collections of short stories to her name when *The Shell Seekers* became an international bestseller and put her on the road to becoming one of the best-loved storytellers of all time.

Her subsequent publications were also hugely successful. Her tales of relationships, of romance, of family secrets – written with great warmth – offer an element of

escapism to what often seem more gentle times, and lent themselves to television adaptations, starting with Emmy Award-winning *The Shell Seekers*, starring Angela Lansbury, in 1989. This was followed in 1998 by *Coming Home* (with Keira Knightley, Emily Mortimer, Peter O'Toole and Joanna Lumley) and its sequel, *Nancherrow*, in 1999. Another television mini-series of *The Shell Seekers* in 2006 starred Vanessa Redgrave.

Angela Lansbury as Penelope Keeling and Sam Wanamaker as Richard Lomax in **The Shell Seekers**

The wide appeal of the stories – so often set in Cornish villages and the Cornish countryside – transcended Britain's shores and since 1993 German film company FFP New Media has turned dozens of them into television dramas, many filmed on location in Cornwall. For a lot of families in Germany, Sunday is 'Rosamunde Pilcher night', the ZDF channel averaging six million viewers tuning in to watch the tales unfold.

After her last novel, *Winter Solstice*, was published in 2000, the author retired. She was awarded an OBE in 2002 and that same year received a British Tourism Award; her popularity continues to give a terrific boost to the number of visitors to Cornwall, including fans flying into Newquay airport from the Continent.

Rosamunde Pilcher died in 2019 but her legacy lives on, through her books, on film, through her world-wide fan base – and, of course, through the evocative landscape and seascape of Cornwall which we explore in *Rosamunde Pilcher's Cornwall*.

Mount Edgcumbe

Torpoint, situated on a peninsula on the estuary of the River Tamar, is one of Cornwall's most easterly towns and a gateway to the county. Close by, at Cremyll, is Mount Edgcumbe. The 865-acre country park can be visited all year round, whilst the fine house – once home to the Earls of Mount Edgcumbe – and its gardens are open to visitors at certain times of year.

In the 15th century, Sir Piers Edgcumbe of Cotehele, near Saltash, acquired the land on which the house was later built, between 1547 and 1550. Several generation of the Edgcumbe family put their mark on the Mount Edgcumbe estate where there is much to enjoy: the house, with its family treasures and works of art; the extensive formal gardens, and the park – incorporating part of the South West Coast Path – where there are plenty of woodland trails to be explored, and a deer park whose inhabitants are descended from fallow deer introduced here by Henry VIII.

Mount Edgcumbe has provided the setting for several German television adaptations of Rosamunde Pilcher's works, including *Eine besondere Liebe* (*A Special Love*) based on one of her short stories.

Mount Edgcumbe

Port Eliot

Inland from Whitsand Bay is the village of St Germans and the stately home of Port Eliot, which has its origins in the 9th century and is a popular spot for filming Rosamunde Pilcher television dramas.

Sir John Soane remodelled the ancestral seat of the Eliot family in the 18th century, and Humphry Repton landscaped the garden and park. Each summer the Port Eliot Festival takes place in the grounds of the estate, with a wonderful mix of artists – writers, poets, musicians and comedians – performing.

Looe

Harbour scenes for *Karussell des Lebens* (*Carousel of Life*) were shot in Looe, a typically Cornish seaside town. As well as the harbourside, the town offers quirky narrow streets and ancient buildings – including the Old Guildhall Museum and Gaol, reflecting the town's history of boatbuilding, fishing and smuggling – which lead to a sandy beach, where visitors may be lucky enough to see a seal offshore. A bronze statue of the town's famous one-eyed grey seal – named Nelson, of course, and who spent much of his long life around the harbour and on Looe Island, a mile off the coast – sits atop Pennyland Rocks at the entrance to the harbour.

Polperro harbour

Polperro

Two of the loveliest ways to travel the short distance from Looe to the picturesque fishing village of Polperro – another filming venue for Rosamunde Pilcher stories – is by boat, or to walk the three-and-a-half-mile stretch of coastal path. The River Pol flows through the traffic-free village to the harbour where, close to the small sandy beach, is Willy Wilcox cave. It is said to be haunted by the 18th-century smuggler of that name who lived in a clifftop cottage here but drowned in the cave whilst hiding from customs officials. More of the history of Polperro can be discovered at its Heritage Museum of Smuggling and Fishing, situated in an old pilchard factory.

Lanhydrock

The beautiful barrel-vaulted ceiling in the Long Gallery at Lanhydrock survived the 1881 fire

Situated between Lostwithiel and Bodmin is the spectacular country estate of Lanhydrock, described by the National Trust – in whose care it has been since 1953 – as 'the grandest house in Cornwall'. Little wonder, then, that it has featured in many Pilcher dramas, amongst them *Im Zweifel für die Liebe* (*Question of Love*) and *Klippen der Liebe* (*Cliffs of Love*).

The Lanhydrock estate, formerly the site of a monastery, was purchased in 1621 by the wealthy Richard Robartes from Truro and the building of a fine family seat began in 1630. The 17th-century gatehouse – still the main entrance to the house and gardens – was retained by George Gilbert Scott when he designed additions to the house in 1857. The gatehouse also survived a fire in 1881 that destroyed much of the house. The rebuild was carried out by Richard Coad, a pupil of Scott, who added such comforts as central heating and electric light. Today's visitors see the house much as it was then, experiencing Victorian life, both upstairs in the opulent family rooms and downstairs in the kitchens and servants' quarters.

The house is set in 1,000 acres; the beautiful gardens offer year-round colour, and the park with its vast, ancient woodlands, riverside paths and cycle trails make for a wonderful family day out.

ST WINNOW

Much of St Winnow Church, a few miles south of Lostwithiel and situated on the east bank of the River Fowey, dates from the 15th century, though its origins are thought to lie in the 7th-century oratory of St Winnoc that was on this site. St Winnow is reached via tree-lined narrow lanes and its idyllic setting has proved popular with film makers, including for German television's *Das Haus an der Küste* (*The House on the Coast*), based on Rosamunde Pilcher's short story *Tea with the Professor*.

Bodmin

The former county town of Cornwall, Bodmin, sits to the east of the wild landscape of Bodmin Moor and has provided a backdrop for *Klippen der Liebe*. The town boasts three railway stations: Bodmin Parkway, Bodmin General and the Bodmin and Wenford Railway. The latter has become a particular favourite for ZDF television adaptations, as well as starring in *Nancherrow* – the British film made for ITV in 1999 as a sequel to *Coming Home* – whose cast included Joanna Lumley as Diana Carey-Lewis, Katie Ryder Richardson as Loveday Carey-Lewis, Susan Hampshire as Miss Catto and Robert Hardy as Viscount Berryann.

BODMIN AND WENFORD RAILWAY

This working heritage railway takes visitors back to the nostalgic days of steam locomotives. The platform is set out in the style of the 1950s, and passengers can take a 13-mile round trip through the Cornish countryside on a steam train, with evocative sights, sounds and smells conjuring up those bygone days.

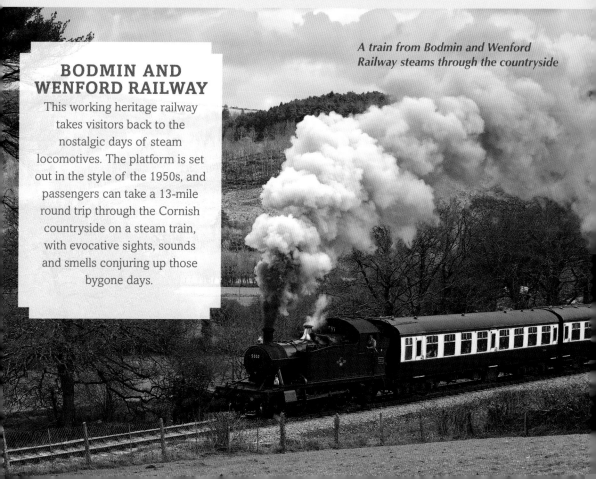

A train from Bodmin and Wenford Railway steams through the countryside

Pencarrow has been home to the same family for nearly 500 years

Pencarrow

Just five miles north of Bodmin is Pencarrow, a country house and gardens which is home to the Molesworth-St Aubyn family. John Molesworth moved here from Northampton in the 1500s when he was appointed auditor of the Duchy of Cornwall and in the mid-18th century his ancestor Sir John Molesworth started to extend the house.

Pencarrow has featured many times in Rosamunde Pilcher adaptations. In *Englischer Wein* (*English Wine*) in 2011 it was Benson Valley Winery; other stories on German TV screens have included *Eine Frage der Ehre* (*A Question of Honour*) and *Wind über der See* (*Wind over the Sea*).

The house and gardens are open to the public for several months each year. The ornate interior of the house is stunning, and filled with antiques and artworks. In the gardens – designed by Sir William Molesworth and his head gardener between 1831 and 1855 – camellias and rhododendrons are a speciality, whilst carpets of bluebells in the woodland in spring are a joy to behold. Peacocks are a familiar sight in the grounds and lend their name to the on-site Peacock cafe, a lovely refreshment stop, offering not-to-be-missed Cornish cream teas.

Fowey

Heading coastward once more, a famous location for filming is the small town situated at the mouth of the river that shares its name: Fowey (pronounced 'Foy'). Pilcher fans may have spotted it in *Karussell des Lebens* (*Carousel of Life*), *Das Haus an der Küste* (*The House on the Coast*) and *Schutzengel* (*Guardian Angel*).

Views of the estuary can be glimpsed along the narrow roads that lead down to the river. The deep-water harbour made Fowey an important port, and today it is still busy with activity from both commercial and leisure boats.

The tiny Fowey Museum is housed in a 15th-century building, one of the oldest in the town, and is packed with artefacts that illustrate the history of the place and its residents. Another writer, Daphne du Maurier, has links to Fowey, and the Daphne du Maurier Literary Centre in South Street has exhibits about her and other authors inspired by the area, including Kenneth Grahame of *The Wind in the Willows* fame.

A view across the estuary to Fowey

A living sculpture in The Lost Gardens of Heligan

In and Around St Austell

In 2000, St Austell – and nearby Mevagissy, a pretty harbour-side village – appeared in *Zeit der Erkenntnis* (*Time of Realization*), based on a Rosamunde Pilcher short story, *The Tree*.

Back in the 18th century, it was the discovery of china clay in the vicinity that changed the landscape and economy of St Austell. Three miles north of the town, at Carthew, a museum at Wheal Martyn Clay Works tells the story of the industry; set in 26 acres, there is much more here besides, and it makes a great day out for families.

Two of Cornwall's most famous visitor attractions are also close to St Austell. The Eden Project at Bodelva showcases plants from around the world and its domes – the Rainforest Biome and the Mediterranean Biome – are an iconic sight. The Lost Gardens of Heligan, at Pentewan, is a 200-acre plant-lovers' paradise which was 'lost' at the outbreak of the First World War and brought to life again in 1990.

—˒— THE SOUTH —˒—

Portscatho

It is unsurprising that Portscatho, on the beautiful Roseland Peninsula, has featured in Rosamunde Pilcher films: positioned on a hill, it commands stunning views for miles along the coast.

Nowadays the village, with its harbour and small beach, is a popular destination for summer visitors, although until around a century ago Portscatho was best known for its pilchard-fishing industry. The sheltered bay was an ideal spot for boats setting out to catch 'Cornish sardines', as pilchards are often called locally.

Trewithen

Ten miles inland from Portscatho is the Trewithen Estate, set in 30 acres of woodland gardens and more than 200 acres of parkland. The house and gardens are open to the public for several months each year.

Phillip Hawkins purchased Trewithen in 1715 and established the estate which has passed down through the generations and still remains in the same family more than 300 years later. The elegant house, much of which dates from c.1770, has starred in Pilcher dramas, including *Blüte des Lebens* (*The Blossom of Life*). This was based on a tale from *The Blue Bedroom & Other Stories*, the author's first collection of short stories which was published in 1985.

Trewithen has one of the loveliest gardens in Cornwall

Trewithen's magnificent gardens were first landscaped in the 18th century by Phillip Hawkins' nephew, and further developed in the 20th century. They offer many highlights, including fine specimens of rhododendrons, camellias and magnolias; a huge and varied collection of trees – several officially declared 'Champion Trees', meaning they have been recognised as the tallest or as having the largest diameter of their species in the country; a wild garden; a camera obscura high above the tree tops; the spectacular Magnolia Fountain – and even the longest lawn in Cornwall!

Truro Cathedral, in the heart of this compact city

Truro

Around eight miles west of Trewithen is Truro, a cathedral city and Cornwall's county town. It sits on the River Truro; formed from the confluence of the Kenwyn and Allen rivers, the inland waterway made Truro an important port from the 14th century.

The county's flourishing mining industry in the 18th and 19th centuries saw elegant townhouses built for the prosperous mine owners; examples of these can still be seen today in the picturesque streets, including the very fine Lemon Street.

The Royal Cornwall Museum in River Street, founded in 1818, gives an excellent insight into Cornish life, its culture and its people, with unique collections and exhibitions.

Truro has long been a centre for filming Pilcher stories, amongst them *Wolken am Horizont* (*Clouds on the Horizon*), *Der lange Weg zum Glück* (*The Long Road to Happiness*), *Zeit der Erkenntnis* (*Time of Realization*) and *Gefährliche Brandung* (*Dangerous Surf*).

TRURO CATHEDRAL

At the heart of the city of Truro is its beautiful triple-spired cathedral, built in the Gothic-Revival style between 1880 and 1910. The origins of the now-widespread Christmas tradition of the Festival of Nine Lessons and Carols are attributed to Truro Cathedral, the inaugural service of that name taking place here on Christmas Eve 1880 at the instigation of the first Bishop of Truro, Edward White Benson (1829–96).

Pendennis Castle, overlooking the River Fal estuary, was built 1540–42

Falmouth

The harbour town of Falmouth, with its beaches, rows of pretty terraced houses and art galleries, has been a location for, amongst several other Pilcher films, *Möwen im Wind* (*Seagulls in the Wind*) and *Evitas Rache* (*Evita's Revenge*).

On Discovery Quay is the National Maritime Museum Cornwall. Set over five floors, visitors are led on a voyage to discover the sea's influence on local history and culture.

Also rich in history is Pendennis Castle, built by Henry VIII on a headland high above Falmouth. Today the fortress is in the care of English Heritage and there is much for families to see and do here.

A LADY PIRATE

The Killigrews were dominant in Falmouth for several centuries. In the 16th century their family home, Arwenack House, was used by Lady Mary Killigrew – who led a double life as a pirate – to store smuggled goods. In 1582, she was sentenced to death for her criminal activities but pardoned by Queen Elizabeth I.

Rosemullion Head

Not far from Falmouth is Rosemullion Head, a promontory with spectacular views. Those who have read *Coming Home* will be familiar with the address of the main character, Judith Dunbar: The Dower House, Rosemullion, a bicycle-ride away from the Nancherrow estate belonging to her friends, the Carey-Lewis family.

Bonython Estate Gardens

A 30-minute drive from Rosemullion Head is Bonython Estate Gardens, a location for Pilcher dramas *Blüte des Lebens* (*The Blossom of Life*), *Sommer des Erwachens* (*Summer of Awakening*) and *Anwälte küsst man nicht* (*Never Kiss a Lawyer*).

The grounds of the estate, whose manor house dates back to 1780, were remodelled and brought back to life when new owners, Richard and Sue Nathan, moved here in 1999. Today visitors can enjoy not only several beautiful gardens – including a walled garden dating from the 18th century – but lakes and streams too, plus refreshments in a thatched tea house.

Cadgwith, a traditional Cornish fishing village

The Lizard Peninsula: Villages and Coves

There are many lovely villages and secluded coves to explore on this 20-mile stretch of dramatic, rocky coastline. One of Cornwall's smallest fishing villages is Cadgwith, which featured in the Pilcher TV film *Ghostwriter*. It is picture-perfect with its cluster of whitewashed cottages, colourful fishing boats and stream wending its way to the sea, where two small, shingle beaches sit either side of a rocky outcrop known as the Todden.

Rounding Britain's southern-most tip at the National Trust's Lizard Point then heading north brings you to Mullion, the largest village on the Lizard. Mullion Cove is a picturesque working harbour protected from wintery gales by the seawalls built in the 1890s. Like Bonython Estate Gardens (situated inland on the peninsula), Mullion Cove featured in *Blüte des Lebens*, *Sommer des Erwachens* and *Anwälte küsst man nicht*, as did Gunwalloe Church Cove, just under three miles away.

Nestled amongst the sand dunes at Gunwalloe Church Cove is St Winwaloe church, which starred in *Zeit der Erkenntnis*. Inside is a screen which, legend claims, was salvaged from a Portuguese ship, the *Saint Anthony*; it sank off Gunwalloe in January 1527 during what was reported to be a 'great and urgent tempest of winds and weather'.

Helston

Six miles inland from Gunwalloe Church Cove is Helston, which has made appearances in *Vollkommen unerwartet* (*Totally Unexpected*) and *Sommer am Meer* (*Summer by the Sea*).

Helston was once one of five 'stannary' towns in Cornwall, whose role was to collect tin coinage to be paid to the Duchy of Cornwall or the Crown. Mined tin, made into ingots, was brought here to be weighed and assayed – whereby a corner (a coin) was cut off to test its quality, before being officially stamped. There is much more of the industrial and social history of the area to be discovered through thousands of fascinating exhibits at Helston's Museum of Cornish Life, housed in the former Market House and Drill Hall.

Many people have heard of Helston's Flora Day, a celebration held in May to chase away winter and welcome in spring. A key event is the 'Furry Dance' which involves local people dancing through the streets, led by the Helston Town Band.

Dancers dressed in their finery process through the streets of Helston on Flora Day

Porthleven

A stormy winter's day in Porthleven

Porthleven, a fishing port with an impressive harbour and three miles of sandy beach, is a favourite holiday destination, despite it being one of the most storm-battered towns in Britain. The 17th-century Ship Inn, which overlooks the historic harbour and was once a haunt of smugglers, appeared in the Pilcher film *Wenn Fische lächeln* (*When Fish Smile*).

—›— THE WEST —›—

Mount's Bay

The magnificent sweep of Mount's Bay stretches from Lizard Point to Gwennap Head, a distance of around 40 miles, and has been a location for *Zeit der Erkenntnis* (*Time of Realization*) as well as *Lichterspiele* (*Light Games*) and *Wind der Hoffnung* (*Wind of Hope*), the latter based on Rosamunde Pilcher's short story *Toby*.

    This part of Cornwall enjoys a varied landscape: rocky cliffs, low hills, sandy beaches, picturesque villages, bustling ports – and a climate ranging from calm summer days to winter gales that threaten ships, evidenced by the number of vessels that have been wrecked here over the centuries.

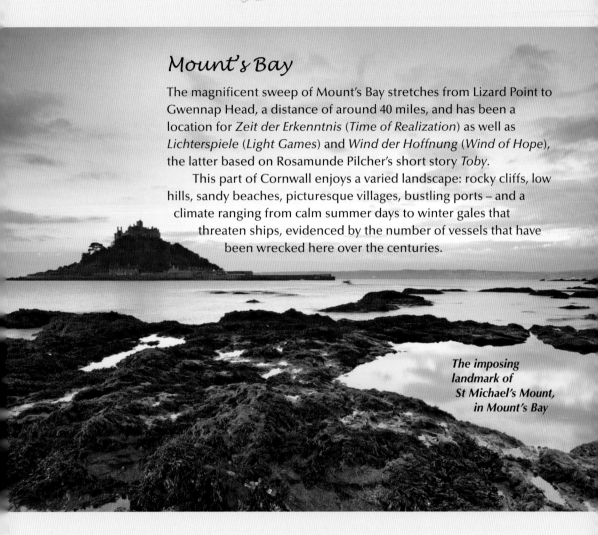

The imposing landmark of St Michael's Mount, in Mount's Bay

Perranuthnoe

Tucked snuggly in the curve of Mount's Bay is Perranuthnoe. This unspoilt village with its 15th-century church and 12th-century Victoria Inn – one of the oldest pubs in Cornwall – is often missed by those hurrying to better-known parts of Cornwall. Its gently sloping beach is known locally as Perran Sands (not to be confused with the beach of the same name at Perranporth on the north coast) and is a lovely spot for families and surfers – but beware the beach disappears at high tide. Filming by German TV crews has taken place at a luxurious local B&B, Endovean Farm, which became The Garden House in *Fast noch verheiratet* (*Almost Unmarried*), adapted from the Rosamunde Pilcher story *The Last Goodbye*.

15

The causeway leading to St Michael's Mount

Marazion

A mile or so from Perranuthnoe is the pretty town of Marazion, with a collection of galleries, gift shops, cafes and a museum. Marazion's safe, sandy beach, lapped by turquoise waters, means it is much enjoyed by families, swimmers and kite-surfers. Most famous of all is its stunning view of the iconic landmark that is St Michael's Mount.

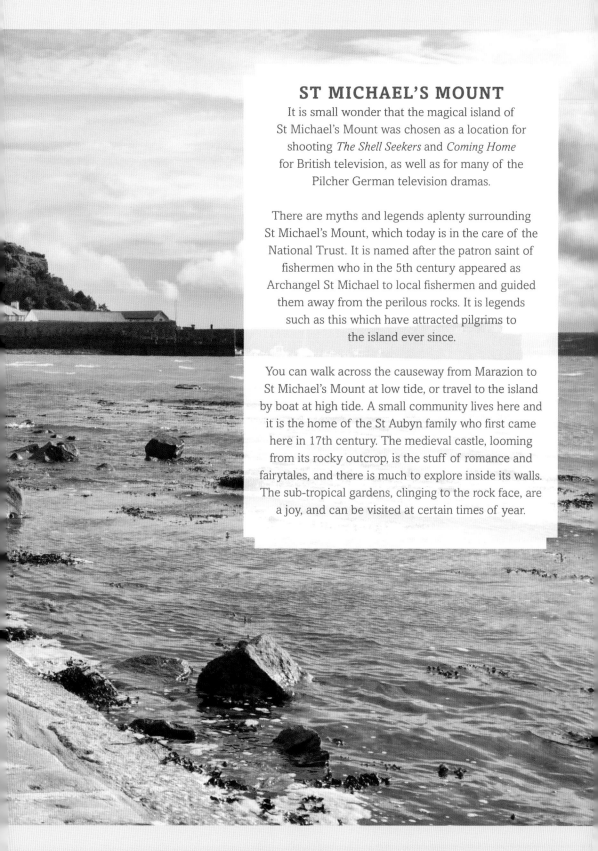

ST MICHAEL'S MOUNT

It is small wonder that the magical island of
St Michael's Mount was chosen as a location for
shooting *The Shell Seekers* and *Coming Home*
for British television, as well as for many of the
Pilcher German television dramas.

There are myths and legends aplenty surrounding
St Michael's Mount, which today is in the care of the
National Trust. It is named after the patron saint of
fishermen who in the 5th century appeared as
Archangel St Michael to local fishermen and guided
them away from the perilous rocks. It is legends
such as this which have attracted pilgrims to
the island ever since.

You can walk across the causeway from Marazion to
St Michael's Mount at low tide, or travel to the island
by boat at high tide. A small community lives here and
it is the home of the St Aubyn family who first came
here in 17th century. The medieval castle, looming
from its rocky outcrop, is the stuff of romance and
fairytales, and there is much to explore inside its walls.
The sub-tropical gardens, clinging to the rock face, are
a joy, and can be visited at certain times of year.

Penzance

Busy, bustling Penzance is Cornwall's most westerly main town and boasts the most temperate climate in the British Isles. Its name is derived from Pen Sans, which is Cornish for 'holy headland' and refers to a chapel founded by early Christians on the promontory to the west of the harbour.

This historic market town features in *Coming Home* – the book and the film – as well as many German TV adaptations. The 17th-century Admiral Benbow pub is full of maritime artefacts reflecting 400 years of shipwrecks along the Cornish coast, and has been in *Sommer des Erwachens* (*Summer of Awakening*).

Rosamunde Pilcher went to St Clare's School in Penzance from the age of eight. Here she met her lifelong friend, Sarah Trembath, who lived between Penzance and Newlyn, and whose parents treated Rosamunde like another daughter. Despite their home being far more modest than the fictional Nancherrow , there is an echo of the relationship between the author and the Trembaths and that enjoyed by Judith Dunbar and the Carey-Lewis family in *Coming Home*.

The architecture of Penzance is worth exploring; particularly striking for its exotic appearance is the Grade I-listed Egyptian House, dating from c.1835

THE NEWLYN INFLUENCE

Penlee House, built in 1865 and set within a lovely park in Penzance, is both a museum and gallery. Here, changing exhibitions often feature works by the Newlyn School, a colony of artists who settled in nearby Newlyn *c.*1880–1940, inspired by the spectacular scenery of the area. The Newlyn Art Gallery itself is in Newlyn, a mile-long walk along the promenade from Penzance. Opened in 1895, it celebrates the long history of artists in west Cornwall. Another venue is The Exchange: housed in what was once the Penzance telephone exchange, it provides a contemporary art space in the town.

Early morning light at Mousehole

Mousehole

The tiny fishing village of Mousehole (pronounced 'Mouzal') is where Welsh author Dylan Thomas spent his honeymoon after marrying Caitlin Macnamara in Penzance, three miles away. Mousehole has been seen in the 1989 film version of *The Shell Seekers*, and in many German TV versions of Pilcher stories, amongst them *Schneesturm im Frühling* (*Snow in April*), based on Rosamunde Pilcher's 1972 book of the same name, and *Sommer am Meer* (*Summer by the Sea*), based on her book *The Empty House*, published in 1973.

Lamorna Cove

A two-mile stroll along the coast from Mousehole leads to the beautiful Lamorna Cove, which has appeared in the same Pilcher films as Mousehole. This was a celebrated spot with the Newlyn School and one of its members, Samuel John Birch (1869–1955), even adopted Lamorna Birch as his name. Examples of his work – much of it inspired by Lamorna Cove – can be seen at Penlee House in Penzance.

DISASTER AT PENLEE POINT

A new lifeboat station was opened at Penlee Point, on the outskirts Mousehole, in 1913. Tragically, on 19 December 1981, the entire crew of eight aboard the lifeboat *Solomon Browne* were lost in a hurricane. Winds reached 100mph (160kph) and waves towered 60 feet (18 metres) in the air as the men attempted to rescue the crew aboard the stricken vessel *Union Star*. All eight on that vessel also died. In honour of those who lost their lives that winter's night, the Christmas lights in Mousehole are turned off for an hour on 19 December each year. Since the tragedy, the Penlee Lifeboat Station has been based in Newlyn.

Porthcurno

Porthcurno has a beautiful sheltered bay, where turquoise waters wash white sands. Perched high on the cliffs overlooking it is the remarkable open-air Minack Theatre, started in the 1930s by Rowena Cade to enable a local drama group to perform Shakespeare's *The Tempest*. The theatre became Rowena's life's work and today the world-famous 750-seat auditorium hosts a varied summer programme. The Exhibition Centre here tells the history of the place, refreshments can be enjoyed in the cafe and there are sub-tropical gardens to visit too.

Some of the cast of Stürmische Begegnung, filmed in Cornwall in 2000

This perfect setting has featured in Pilcher films *Lichterspiele* (*Light Games*) and *Zeit der Erkenntnis* (*Time of Realization*), in which soprano Sarah Brightman made a guest appearance singing *Scarborough Fair*.

Porthgwarra

A little over a mile from Porthcurno along the South West Coast Path is Porthgwarra, which lays claim to being England's most south-westerly cove. Although privately owned by the Molesworth-St Aubyn family, visitors are welcome. With its rock pools, caves and a slipway that reveals Porthgwarra's past as a busy fishing village, this secluded place proved a natural choice for filming *The Shell Seekers*, starring Angela Lansbury, and *Coming Home*.

The wooded cliffs and the heather and gorse moorland above the cove teem with birdlife and make this one of Britain's best birdwatching sites, with many rare species seen here.

Gwennap Head

Like Porthgwarra, this headland is another wonderful spot for birdwatchers. Out in the ocean you may see other wildlife: dolphins, porpoises, basking sharks and, if you are really lucky, whales.

This is a scenic but dangerous rocky stretch of water and keeping lookout is the National Coastwatch, whose volunteers oversee various sections of the UK coastline. The National Coastwatch station at Gwennap Head became the Sea Rescue helicopter station in the German Pilcher drama *Zu hoch geflogen* (*Flew Too High*).

Around nine miles offshore is Wolf Rock Lighthouse, an important beacon for ships in the treacherous waters of the Celtic Sea where many ships have come to grief over hundreds of years. Closer to shore is Runnel Stone Reef, a popular site with experienced divers wishing to seek out the wrecks when conditions allow.

Land's End

The Land's End peninsula stretches all the way from Penzance on its southern side to St Ives on the north coast, a distance of around 40 miles along the South West Coast Path.

Land's End itself is the peninsula's most famous landmark. This is a designated Area of Outstanding Natural Beauty, with over 100 acres of incredible scenery to enjoy, as well as all that is on offer at the Land's End Visitor Centre.

Close to Land's End is Britain's most westerly point of all: Sennen Cove. At low tide its crescent-shaped Whitesands Beach joins the neighbouring Gwenver Beach, which slopes steeply into the Atlantic. The mile-long stretch of sand that is created, washed by the ocean's swell, is a big attraction for surfers.

Unsurprisingly, the stunning landscape of Land's End has appeared in both the 1989 and 2006 films of *The Shell Seekers*, and several other Rosamunde Pilcher adaptions, amongst them *Stürmische Begegnung* (*The Day of the Storm*), *Sommer am Meer* (*Summer by the Sea*) and *Liebe am Horizont* (*Love on the Horizon*), the latter based on a short story, *Dear Tom*, written in 1954 under the pseudonym Jane Fraser.

Land's End

Cape Cornwall

The word 'cape' is usually applied to a piece of land jutting out between two great bodies of water and, seven miles north of Land's End, is Britain's only place to bear that title: Cape Cornwall. Until around 200 years ago, this distinctive rocky promontory was believed to be Cornwall's most westerly point and therefore thought to be 'land's end'. From this rugged, lonely place, which is a great attraction for seabirds, there is nothing but water until the coast of Labrador and Newfoundland in Canada.

A chimney stack from the tin mine that operated at Cape Cornwall from 1838 to 1883 still remains as a landmark. Tunnels from the mine ran beneath the sea to the twin rocks known as The Brisons, a mile offshore and the site of several shipwrecks.

Cape Cornwall, gifted to the National Trust in 1987, has appeared in *Sommer am Meer* (*Summer by the Sea*), *Schneesturm im Frühling* (*Snow in April*) and *Lichterspiele* (*Light Games*) which was based on Rosamunde Pilcher's novel *Another View*, published in 1969.

The Mermaid of Zennor, a 1900 watercolour by J. R. Weguelin

Zennor

East of the Tin Coast (see panel) is Zennor, another filming location for *Sommer am Meer*. Farming, fishing and mining were all important industries here, as was quarrying. Granite from a local quarry was used to build much of St Ives, further along the coast. Today, however, tourism brings trade to the village, where the 13th-century pub, the Tinners Arms, offers a warm welcome and a slice of history. It was built to accommodate the masons who were building St Senara's Church, which is legendary for the mermaid carved on a 600-year-old wooden seat. The story goes that chorister Matthew Trewella sang so beautifully that a mermaid, Morveren, made her way to the church to hear him. Enchanted by her beauty, he followed her to nearby Pendour Cove where the pair disappeared into the sea. Some say they can be heard singing beneath the waves …

THE TIN COAST

The stretch of coastline between Cape Cornwall and Pendeen Lighthouse is known as the Tin Coast, a World Heritage Site reflecting the area's tin-mining history. Like Cape Cornwall itself, Botallack Mines and Levant Mine and Beam Engine are also in the care of the National Trust and well worth visiting. Geevor Tin Mine at Pendeen, a working mine until 1991, also offers an excellent day out, with its interactive museum, underground tunnels for exploring and the chance to have a go at panning for minerals.

Levant Mine on
the Tin Coast

St Ives

St Ives, just three miles from where Rosamunde Pilcher was born, is where she spent much of her childhood. Her mother, Helen, belonged to the Art Club of St Ives and her children – Rosamunde and her older sister, Lalage – were encouraged in their artistic talents, always 'making something, painting or working on a play'. It is little wonder that the place she knew so well become the fictional town of Porthkerris in her novels. (There is, however, a real Porthkerris: a secluded cove on the Lizard where a diving school is based.)

The beauty of the region and special quality of light that St Ives enjoys is unlike anywhere else in Cornwall and has drawn artists to the town for over 200 years. There are many art studios and galleries here, the most famous being Tate St Ives, opened in 1993. Also in St Ives are the studios of two of the most influential artists of the 20th century: the Barbara Hepworth Museum and Sculpture Garden, and the Leach Pottery. What a marvellous picture is conjured up in *The Shell Seekers* when Lawrence Stern speaks of how people would come to paint not only the obvious scenes of the bay and boats, but also 'the warmth of the sun' and 'the colour of the wind'.

The beaches where Rosamunde Pilcher played as a child, the 18th-century Tregenna Castle (now a hotel and holiday resort) and the tiny St Nicholas Chapel, surrounded on three sides by the ocean and once used by customs officials as a lookout point for smugglers, all feature in many of the TV versions of her works, including *Wolken am Horizont* (*Clouds on the Horizon*) and *Morgens stürmisch, abends Liebe* (*Storm in the Morning, Love in the Evening*), which premiered on the ZDF channel in 2019 and was adapted from the short story *All for the Best*. In her book *Another View*, Rosamunde Pilcher based her fictional Sliding Tackle pub on the 14th-century Sloop Inn on the harbourside at St Ives, still a favourite haunt of artists and fishermen.

Summer in St Ives; St Nicholas Chapel can be seen at the highest point

Lelant

Between St Ives and Hayle is Lelant, the village where Rosamunde Pilcher was born and where, in her evocative words, 'the wind smelt of salt'. The gardens of the fine Edwardian house in which she lived, The Elms (now renamed The Firs and offering elegant bed and breakfast accommodation), run down to a little branch-line railway station. This is reminiscent of the location of Riverview House in *Coming Home*, where Judith Dunbar spent her early years and travelled by train to and from Porthkerris School. Indeed, Lelant featured in the 1998 British TV dramatisation of that novel.

It was at St Uny Church in Lelant that Rosamunde married Graham Pilcher in December 1946. The young couple met at a party when he, an officer in the Black Watch, was staying in St Ives with his grandmother while he recovered from severe war wounds.

A funeral was filmed in the cemetery of the church in *Land der Sehnsucht* (*Land of Longing*), the story taken from the author's first book published under her own name in 1955: *A Secret to Tell*.

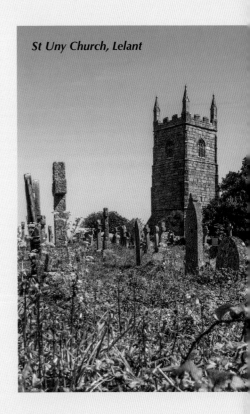

St Uny Church, Lelant

PARADISE PARK

Paradise Park, a family-run wildlife sanctuary near Hayle, was one of the venues where *Schlangen im Paradies* (*Snakes in Paradise*), adapted from one of Rosamunde Pilcher's stories, was filmed. At the centre of the park is Glanmor House, built for the Harveys of Hayle, who in the 19th century were world-renowned for making beam engines to pump water out of mines, including local tin and copper mines. During the film shoot it became the zoo office and some of the zoo keepers appeared as extras in that particular episode.

Gwithian Beach

A four-mile walk along the coast from the Hayle Estuary brings you to Gwithian Beach, a favoured site for filming Pilcher tales, including *Klippen der Liebe* (*Cliffs of Love*), *Möwen im Wind* (*Seagulls in the Wind*), *Gefährliche Brandung* (*Dangerous Surf*) and *Über den Wolken* (*Above the Clouds*).

Gwithian's golden beach – backed by the Towans, a Cornish word for sand dunes – has rock pools and caves visible at a low tide, making it a great destination for families, whilst the constant swell of the ocean means it is perfect for surfers all year round.

Much of the area is dedicated as a Site of Special Scientific Interest and there are several local nature reserves here. Upton Towans reserve, in the care of the Cornwall Wildlife Trust, is a wonderful habitat for, in particular, birds, butterflies … and even glow-worms. Upton Towans was also once the sight of a dynamite factory – the National Explosives Works – which was founded towards the end of the 19th century; ruins of the buildings can still be seen.

Godrevy Point

Another mile or so along the coast is Godrevy Point, used in the same German TV adaptations as Gwithian Beach, and also appearing in *Wenn Fische lächeln* (*When Fish Smile*). The scenic Godrevy Point can also be seen in the 1998 British TV version of *Coming Home*, in which Peter O'Toole and Joanna Lumley played husband and wife Edgar and Diana Carey-Lewis.

Godrevy's vast, sandy beach, in the care of the National Trust, is ideal for families and surfers, whilst the headlands are a paradise for birdwatchers. A short distance from Godrevy Point is Mutton Cove. Although virtually inaccessible as it is enclosed by sheer cliffs (and cut off at high tide), the beauty of this place is that it is the year-round home to a large colony of grey seals; binoculars are recommended to get a good view of them.

Seals on the beach at Mutton Cove

GODREVY LIGHTHOUSE

Just offshore is Godrevy Lighthouse, which marks a dangerous reef known as The Stones. Virginia Woolf used to holiday in the area and it is thought that this lighthouse was the inspiration behind her 1927 novel *To the Lighthouse*, despite the story being set in Scotland.

The distinctive white octagonal lighthouse is situated on Godrevy Island where, in 1649, a ship was wrecked. It had been carrying garments belonging to the executed King Charles I, in an effort by those who considered his execution a martyrdom to send his possessions abroad as relics for safekeeping. Many other ships met their fate here but the lighthouse was not built until 1859, following the loss of all on board the SS *Nile* in 1854.

St Agnes Head

The views from the rugged clifftops of St Agnes Head, high above the Atlantic Ocean, are some of the most spectacular on this section of Cornwall's north coast. Its wild, natural beauty has been seen in films and dramas of all types, including Rosamunde Pilcher's *Nancherrow*, made for British TV, in which the sagas of the lives of those who are part of, or involved with, the Carey-Lewis family – first introduced in Rosamunde Pilcher's book *Coming Home* – continue. St Agnes Head also appears as a backdrop in many episodes of her stories adapted for German TV.

Amongst the gorse and heather of the heathland that crowns St Agnes Head, the remains of engine houses that once pumped water out of the tin and copper mines are a familiar part of the landscape. They are a stark reminder that Cornwall was once one of the UK's biggest producers of these minerals, but by the late 19th century the industry was in serious decline with increased competition from foreign imports. Today the St Agnes district is dedicated as a Cornish Mining World Heritage Site.

Towanroath Shaft engine house, part of the Wheal Coates mine

Chapel Porth and Wheal Coates

Two particular sites close to St Agnes Head that will be familiar with fans of Pilcher television films are Chapel Porth beach and Wheal Coates, both in the care of the National Trust. At low tide the vast expanse of Chapel Porth's sandy beach is exposed, with rock pools and caves ripe for exploring. The powerful waves make for good surfing – but it is important to know that the beach disappears at high tide.

Wheal Coates, overlooking Chapel Porth, was a working mine from 1802 to 1899, and re-opened, briefly, between 1911 and 1913. There are three engine houses here, the most iconic being the Grade II-listed Towanroath Shaft. This is good walking country and making your way to Wheal Coates evokes a tremendous sense of the history of the area.

Newquay

Around 12 miles east of St Agnes Head is Newquay, named for the 'new quay' built in 1429 where the harbour now stands. The introduction of passenger trains to the town in the Victorian era saw the growth of this former fishing village as a holiday destination and the arrival of surfing as a sport on British shores in the 1960s saw a further expansion. Today it is one of Cornwall's most popular seaside resorts, the fine beaches attracting tens of thousands of holidaymakers every year.

Scenes from *Nancherrow* were shot in Newquay, including on the headland known as Towan Head where there are fantastic views from an old lookout building. Filming for several German titles has also happened in Newquay, often using its fine beaches. At Towan Beach, to the east of Towan Head, is an island, connected to the mainland by a suspension bridge, with a house – built in 1910 for an eccentric recluse – which is available to rent as a unique holiday retreat.

Two of the most charmingly named beaches that feature in Pilcher dramas are Little Fistral Beach, a little to the north of the bigger and busier Fistral Beach, and Lusty Glaze Beach. Lusty Glaze, nestled in a sheltered cove, is privately owned, though public access is permitted. There is a fabulous restaurant here, picturesque beach huts and an activity centre for those seeking sporting adventure.

Before Lusty Glaze became a bathing resort in the 1920s, there was an iron ore mine here, this having been one of few coastal beaches rich in that mineral. The name Lusty Glaze is said to be Cornish for 'a place to view blue boats', a reference to the small blue boats that were used to transport the ore to Newquay Harbour.

Actors Barbara Wussow and Albert Fortell filming Englischer Wein *(English Wine); the suspension bridge leading to the island above Towan Beach is in the background*

Bedruthan Steps

Between Newquay and Padstow are Bedruthan Steps. Legend has it that the steps – three huge stacks of slate – were used by a giant called Bedruthan as a shortcut across the bay.

As well as being a Site of Special Scientific Interest, in 2014 this National Trust site was granted 'Dark Sky' status, meaning it is free from light pollution and accessible to the public – though visitors should be prepared for a steep walk down to the small beach. The breath-taking views from the cliffs make this a popular film location and aerial shots have appeared in several Pilcher dramas.

Bedruthan Steps

Padstow

Padstow has been the scene for many Pilcher tales, including *Coming Home* for British television and German television's *Zerrissene Herzen* (*Torn Hearts*), based on the short story *Amita* from *The Blue Bedroom* collection.

Long before celebrity chef Rick Stein put Padstow on the map as a destination for foodies, this charming fishing harbour was a major port, servicing the mining and quarrying industries that were once so important to the area. The history of the town can be explored in depth at Padstow Museum, where interactive displays bring the past to life for visitors.

The waters around Padstow can be dangerous. At the mouth of the Camel estuary is the notorious Doom Bar sandbank which, if legend is to be believed, was created as the dying curse of a mermaid shot by a sailor; it has seen countless shipwrecks. However, there are lovely beaches close by. Boat trips are a great way to see the coastline, including the foot-ferry that travels across the River Camel to Rock.

Port Isaac

It is around 16 miles by car from Padstow to Port Isaac, but about half that distance if you take the foot-ferry, and walk from Rock.

Although Port Isaac is perhaps best known to British television viewers as the place where the fictional Doc Martin lives and works, this pretty fishing village also starred in *The Shell Seekers*. Leading down to the harbour, its winding, narrow streets are flanked by typical Cornish cottages and the village boasts one of the narrowest thoroughfares in Britain; although officially called Temple Bar, it is more affectionately known as Squeezy Belly Alley.

Squeezy Belly Alley, Port Isaac

PRIDEAUX PLACE

Prideaux Place in Padstow has been home to the Prideaux-Brune family since 1592. This stately home, set in magnificent grounds with views as far as Bodmin Moor, was inherited by Peter Prideaux-Brune in 1988, who has taken cameo roles in numerous Rosamunde Pilcher dramas made here for German TV. These include: *Das Geheimnis der weissen Taube* (*The Secret of the White Dove*); *Der Doktor und drei Frauen* (*A Doctor and Three Women*); *Die Frau auf der Klippe* (*The Woman on the Cliff*); *Wahlversprechen und andere Lügen* (*Promises and Lies*); and *Das Gespenst von Cassley* (*The Ghost of Cassley*).

The house and grounds are open to visitors at certain times of the year, and all year round for group visits by appointment.

BUDE CASTLE HERITAGE CENTRE

Now a heritage centre, Bude Castle was once the home of one of the town's most famous sons, the Victorian inventor Sir Goldsworthy Gurney, best known in the early part of the 19th century for his steam-powered road vehicles.

Bude

A 30-mile stretch of the South West Coast Path leads from Port Isaac to Bude, the final destination on this exploration of Rosamunde Pilcher's Cornwall. The harbour and canal here were once particularly important for the transportation of sand and coal but the coming of the railway in 1897 started its popularity as a seaside resort. There are plenty of independent shops and eateries in Bude but the biggest draw for families and surfers are the wide, sandy beaches.

Summerleaze Beach in the town is hugely popular, as is Crooklets Beach – and especially so with surfers. A two-mile walk north at low tide brings you to a National Trust beach at Sandymouth Bay, known for its spectacular cliff and rock formations. At low tide the wreck of a Portuguese steamship, the SS *Belem*, which became stranded in thick fog in 1917, can be seen.

Around three miles south of Bude is Widemouth Bay, where filming of *Das Ende eines Sommers* (*The End of Summer*) – based on Rosamunde Pilcher's book of the same name – took place. This beautiful beach, which enjoys the full force of the Atlantic's wind and waves, is a fitting end to this journey, for even in her later years Rosamunde Pilcher would return to Cornwall, where she still enjoyed 'walking on those lovely beaches'.

Sunset over the rocky outcrop known as Black Rock at Widemouth Bay, near Bude

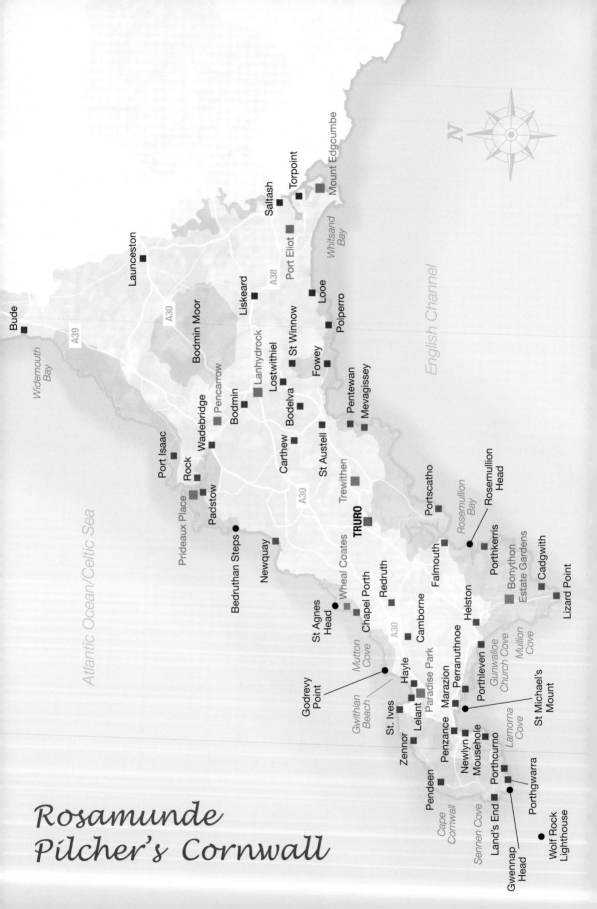

Rosamunde
Pilcher's Cornwall